© Copyright 1989 Omnibus Press
(A Division of Book Sales Limited)

ISBN 0.7119.1960.7 Order No. OP45590

Exclusive distributors:
Book Sales Limited
8/9 Frith Street,
London W1V 5TZ, UK.
Music Sales Corporation
225 Park Avenue South,
New York, NY 10003, USA.
Music Sales Pty Limited
120 Rothschild Avenue,
Rosebery, NSW 2018, Australia.
To the Music Trade only:
Music Sales Limited.
8/9 Frith Street,
London W1V 5TZ, UK.

Edited by Chris Charlesworth
Art Direction by Tony Foo
Designed by Monica Chrysostomou
Picture research by Debbie Dorman

Picture Credits:
London Features International, Pictorial Press and All Action.

Typeset by Capital Setters
Printed in England by J.B. Offset Printers (Marks Tey) Limited,
Marks Tey, Colchester, Essex.

Acknowledgements
This one's for the boys in the band, Bob 'Lauder' Kelly and
Michael 'Hold your coat, sir?' McDonagh-Jones; for every
girl who's ever worn a paisley mini-skirt, and for
Katya Pendill, the most complicated girl I know.

Special thanks (for info, insights and general support) to:
Chris Charlesworth, Debbie Dorman and Caroline Watson
at Omnibus, Patrick Humphries and Sue Parr, John and
Gael Whelan, Igor Goldkind and Steve MacManus at CRISIS,
brothers Dave and Sean, Vanessa and John, Charles Shaar
Murray and Alan 'the Baald' Price. And Jim: 'thank you for the
days' in D.C. Goodnight,
Vera; sweet dreams . . .

Peter K. Hogan, London/July 1989.

Omnibus Press
London/New York/Sydney

□ The first time I ever heard Susanna Hoffs sing, I thought I'd died and gone to heaven. Of course, it didn't hurt that she was singing one of my favourite songs – 'I'll Keep It With Mine', the love song Bob Dylan wrote for Nico back when she was still the Ice Goddess of Warhol's Factory – but what amazed me at the time was that I *instantly* preferred Hoffs' version to those I already knew and loved: Nico's, Fairport Convention's (with Sandy Denny singing) and Dylan's own version (complete with the unique Zimmerman plunketty-klunk piano style, which didn't *officially* surface until the 1985 retrospective boxed set 'Biograph'). Hoff's voice had a plaintive, haunting quality that was impossible to resist; long before I ever saw a photograph of her I knew she was beautiful.

At the time (late 1982), I was working for Rough Trade Records, the leading light of the English indie scene, and the small American label Llama had offered us an album called 'Rainy Day' to release in Britain. Hoffs' cover of the Dylan song opened the album, which turned out to be a compilation of cover versions of sixties psychedelia performed by musicians drawn from a number of new, sixties-obsessed guitar groups: The Dream Syndicate, The Three O'Clock, The Rain Parade . . . and The Bangles. Collectively dubbed 'the paisley underground' by The Three O'Clock's Michael Quercio, these bands seemed like a real ray of hope at a time when fey haircuts and rampant synthesizers were dominating the pop charts (at the expense of tunes, talent etc), and I'd listened to most of their recorded output . . . but I'd never heard of The Bangles. Still, I was impressed enough by their contribution to 'Rainy Day' (both Susanna and Vicki Peterson provided backing vocals on several tracks, and Susanna also took lead vocals on a creditable version of another song associated with Nico, The Velvet Underground's 'I'll Be Your Mirror') to track down their début mini-album, 'The Bangles', and give it a spin.

And I was really disappointed. Most of The Bangles trademarks were present: there was obviously a strong Beatles influence (with shades of The Monkees thrown in); there were jangly guitars and thrashing drums, bitter-sweet harmonies (far more ragged than of late) – all the ingredients were there but one. There were no real tunes. It was all filler and no singles, pleasant but unmemorable; so I promptly forgot all about The Bangles for several years . . . until they came blasting out of the radio to remind me just how much I'd liked Susanna's voice in the first place.

□ **THE BANGLES STORY** actually began two decades earlier in Los Angeles, with the birth of **VICKI PETERSON** on January 11, 1961 (or '62, depending on who you believe). A year later, Vicki's sister **DEBBI** was born, and the two grew up in Northridge, a small town in the San Fernando Valley. Their father Milton was an engineer, their mother Jeanne a former model who later worked for California congressman Glenn Anderson. Both Peterson parents were music fans, and the radio was always on; Vicki remembers all four Peterson children being woken up to see The Beatles on the **Ed Sullivan TV Show.** "I always wanted to perform," she would later recall. "My parents have home movies of me aged three, dancing, bumping into tables, getting black eyes." When she was seven, her parents bought her her first (plastic) guitar, and she began to bash out old folk songs like 'Tom Dooley'. By the age of nine she was composing her own songs.

□ The Beatles would remain a lifetime love for Vicki, and by the time she'd reached her teens and was spending all her time playing her imitation Rickenbacker guitar in her room, her musical taste in general was running to the sounds of the sixties rather than the seventies. She'd formed her first group – "a female Simon And Garfunkel" – with her best friend Amanda (another guitarist) by the age of 15, and "was writing in the style of Joni Mitchell, but my true love was The Hollies and The Beatles." In other words, harmonic folkie rock. When she decided that her new band needed a drummer, she simply drafted in sister Debbi by buying her a drumkit. Given Vicki's obsession with vocal harmonies, it was an inevitable alliance, as Debbi later told **New Musical Express**'s Mat Snow: "Vicki tells me that I always used to sit in the back of the car, a big Buick station wagon, when I was three-years-old, and boys would come on the radio and I'd bop-shoo-wop the background parts. I'm a born background singer!"

□ Far quieter than her sister, Debbi had comparatively few friends at school. "I'd look at Vicki and she was always the most popular one – she'd be cheerleader and I was just a drill team person. And later . . . I wanted to be in her band *so* badly. I said, 'I'll do anything – I'll even play *drums*! '" Debbi later repaid her sister for the drumkit with money she'd earned through working at McDonald's ("one of the worst experiences of my life"). The girls' ensemble began life as Crista Galli ("a small bone at the back of the head") before changing its name to Aishi (Vicki: "We couldn't stand having a name that you

"You can look around you and pretend it's 1966, that's a nice fantasy. But it's not 1966, it's been done. Which is kind of the sadness about this whole Sixties revival. Music *was* great then, and none of us was old enough to appreciate it on a mature level. So when you get older, you can get stuck in a time warp – 'Nothing good has happened since 1966.' We actually have friends who say that. That's sad."
□ Vicki

"Vicki wants to bring back bell-bottoms. Not those *really* flared bell-bottoms, but bell-bottoms like Cher wore. You know Sonny and Cher? Vicki's also mad about Cher bells – the sort you wear round your neck. She wants to start a Cher appreciation society."
□ Susanna

could pronounce easily. Aishi means 'life' and 'positive vibes'"), then The Muze, then The Fans, followed by Shanti ('peace'), Those Girls and the memorably christened KooKoo And The DooDooHeads. Other musicians came and went (Amanda quit at college to concentrate on her archaeology studies), but the Peterson girls kept on rehearsing; Vicki was determined not to give up. "I never doubted that the band would work," she later told **Rolling Stone**'s Susan Orlean, "which makes me totally irrational."

☐ Vicki and Debbi pursued their dream even after leaving their Catholic School, Our Lady Of Lourdes. Vicki attended college at UCLA as an English major, while Debbi (much to her parents' horror) worked in a succession of menial clerical jobs. In 1980 the sisters were sharing an apartment in Hollywood with the third girl in their band, and witnessed the tired LA

music scene become rejuvenated as it finally caught up with punk and the 'new wave'. And suddenly it was okay for girls to be musicians – several important new groups contained female players, like Talking Heads' Tina Weymouth. Blondie's Debbie Harry had re-invented herself as an icon and became (briefly) a rock archetype in the process, and wholly female bands – The Slits and The Bodysnatchers (later The Bellestars) in England, The Go-Go's in America – had transcended the girls-can-be-as-bad-as-boys pantomime that had limited earlier all-female outfits like Fanny or The Runaways. Something was going on, and Vicki wanted to be a part of it. "There were all these bands, like The Go-Go's and The Knack, that were focusing attention on LA," Vicki later recalled, "and I was afraid it would all leave me behind." It might have done, if the Petersons hadn't met Susanna Hoffs.

□ **SUSANNA LEE HOFFS** was born on January 17, 1962, the daughter of a psychoanalyst father (Joshua) and a painter/filmmaker mother (Tamar), and grew up with her two brothers in West LA, in an atmosphere of gentle bohemia – an "atheist, intellectual, creative world," as she'd later describe it. "They're very progressive; we had no closed topics in our house. They had this vision of coming to California and having this very Utopian family where all the kids would be artists and they, as parents, would let us say what we wanted, swear if we wanted to, see X-rated films, ask questions about sex and so on.

"When I was a kid, people used to say, 'No wonder you're crazy – your father's a psychoanalyst!' I used to say, 'No, no; kids of psychoanalysts are *normal*.' But now I say, 'Yeah! It *does* give you a different perspective on reality because Freud is God!' It really sets you apart from other people when you're raised with psychology as your religion."

Music entered her life early on, "From when I was three or four-years-old. I loved listening to The Beatles and things, all the sixties stuff. My mother was a really 'hip mum', wearing mini-skirts, boots and lacy tops. She would bring home records for my brothers and I – that was the beginning. I got my first guitar when I was something like eight years old. We all had guitars. My brothers and I would play and sing together, and my uncle who played with Linda Ronstadt and Joni Mitchell would come over and give us lessons."

She studied ballet from the age of five, and was still studying it – along with theatre and film and painting – while attending college at Berkeley, where she also rediscovered music and began to think about playing in a band, "'cause the world of dance is so very restricted. I needed a lot more control with what was happening with my life." Her first band (which included both her brothers and boyfriend David Roback, later of The Rain Parade) was called The Psychiatrists. It didn't last long. "It was an imaginary band, very, um, *conceptual*. We were going to do things like have 50-minute performances because psychiatrists' hours are 50-minutes long."

"Some of my friends weren't very supportive," Susanna later told the **NME**'s Mat Snow. "I was so into rock at Berkeley; I'd go to Patti Smith concerts and saw The Sex Pistols and all those bands, and I would want to be where they were. And I'd say that to my friends and they'd say, 'How dare you even *assume* that you could ever be on-stage?' We were just so into idolising rock musicians and the whole thing that it was *audacious* of me to think that I wanted to do that.

"In high school I'd been playing guitar and singing and dancing and doing theatre and film and all that stuff from day one. But college is where I really moved into more avant-garde rock fantasies – Patti Smith and rediscovering The Velvet Underground. I graduated, but I just played rock 'n' roll in my room to tapes. I was a total closet . . . I mean, I always tell people, 'What is your definition of rock 'n' roll?' Rock 'n' roll is sitting alone in your room listening to your stereo or playing guitar or whatever. It's a totally *personal* thing.''

> "I really relate to old hippies. They seem to have this
> focus on the inner things, the inner beauty
> as opposed to, say, plastic surgery . . . breast
> implants, nose jobs, cheek implants, whatever."
> □ Susanna

□ In 1981 Susanna graduated from Berkeley, and
placed an ad in a Los Angeles weekly newspaper, in
quest of possible bandmates. She also answered an
ad placed by a girl whose room-mates had just fired
her from their band; Susanna didn't get on with the
girl, but found herself immediately drawn to the girl's
room-mates, Vicki and Debbi Peterson. "It was
amazing," Vicki would later say. "It was pretty much
an instantaneous thing with Susanna." "It was weird,"
Susanna confirms. "I'd say, 'I love the Grass Roots,
I love The Hollies, I love Love with Arthur Lee.' It
was just so weird they knew all those groups." And so
The Bangles were born, virtually overnight.

But though they shared a love for tight vocal
harmonies and the music of the sixties – especially
The Byrds, The Buffalo Springfield and The Mamas
And Papas – it wasn't all smooth sailing. "It was really
scary," Susanna recalled later. "I remember talking
to Vicki in the kitchen about a week after we decided
to form the band, and I suddenly got these butterflies
in my stomach. It was like I'd married a stranger. She
was talking about her background and everything. It
was so different from mine that although I really liked
her, it was just a strange sensation." Still, the good
Catholic girls and the boho wild child got on well
enough to start playing together in Susanna's garage.

At first they called themselves The Colours ("with a
'u'," remembers Debbi, "very British"), then Susanna
discovered an old copy of **Esquire** magazine
featuring some of the sixties' more outlandish
hairstyles, and the girls promptly became The
Supersonic Bangs, which was then shortened to The
Bangs. "We liked the double-entendre of the name,"
said Susanna. "You can read a lot into it. There was
something kind of gutsy about it."

So the girls practised in the garage, Susanna taking
rhythm guitar and Vicki lead. They drafted in a bass
player called Annette Zilinskas and started playing
small clubs: The Topanga Corral, Club 88 and HJ's.
They also hung out at Rodney Bingenheimer's English
Disco, where the ambience consisted of "platforms,
pineapple hairdos, bad make-up and quaaludes."

□ Vicki: "We didn't issue a lot of demo tapes to record companies and sit back. We wanted to build up a following from the ground floor, by getting out there and playing. We've played all the dives and gone on-stage in some really horrible places where nice girls aren't supposed to go.

"We were never in with the trends. We never played hardcore music. We never played rockabilly music. We never played power pop. We never fitted into a slot."

Vicki handled the club bookings; between earnings and their savings they managed to scrape up enough cash to finance recording their own single, 'Getting Out Of Hand'; it cost them $800, and 1,000 copies were pressed and released on their own Downkiddie Records in 1981. The girls even packed the singles themselves in (you guessed it) Susanna's garage. The indie approach and having their own label was important to them – despite the lack of hard cash, they had freedom *and* control. [As late as 1985, there was talk of Downkiddie being re-activated as a home for small bands that the girls liked. They even planned to release unreleased tracks by The Salvation Army (an early incarnation of The Three O'Clock) on Downkiddie, but nothing came of it.]

□ It was at this point that they came to the attention of Miles Copeland, manager of The Police and owner of IRS Records. Copeland, with Mike Gormley, his partner in the LA Personal Direction management company, attended a Bangs show and was impressed with what he saw. He'd previously struck gold with The Go-Go's, an all-girl pop group who cut two huge hit albums before breaking up (which in itself launched the solo careers of ex-Go-Go's Belinda Carlisle and Jane Wiedlin), but – impressive as Copeland's credentials were, Vicki was highly dubious: the last thing The Bangs wanted was to become a "poor man's Go-Go's."

Comparisons between the two groups were inevitable, especially since The Go-Go's star was then riding high. "But then," says Gormley, "we saw them not as a pop band but a rock band whose members were women." Nonetheless, The Bangs were still dubious, and took a tape recorder along to their first meeting with the management company. "We were the ultimate of trying to do everything as carefully as possible," Vicki recalls, "and we'd avoided anything even smelling like a manager, up until then." In the end, the girls signed a management contract with LAPD, with the promise of recording an EP for Copeland's Faulty Products label. In the event, the mini-album – which was cut and mixed in three

"When I first started listening to Joni Mitchell I was 13 – like this little girl hearing an adult woman sing about her lovers and herself, her emotions. How her lover is like a little boy and he wants her to be his mother. At the time, I didn't understand any of it, I just loved the harmonies. Now I'm a woman I'm going back to it again and it means something new to me. I can appreciate the lyrics in a new way. I've *had* the experiences that she talked about when she was writing those records."
□ Susanna

days flat – lay on the shelf for six months as Faulty Products collapsed, and was eventually released on Copeland's other label, IRS. At around this time, The Bangs were also filmed for a cameo appearance in **The Haircut**, a short film made by Susanna's mother, which starred John Cassavetes (an old friend of the Hoffs family) and which is still doing the rounds on the arthouse circuit. Family ties are strong with all The Bangles: the Petersons' parents later worked with The Bangles fanclub, and their older sister became the band's accountant.

□ Copeland also signed The Bangs to appear – at five days' notice – as opening act on the 1982 Beat tour of the USA. On the eve of the tour The Bangs discovered that they had to change their name; another group called The Bangs was threatening them with a lawsuit (ironically, The Beat themselves had had to change their name to The English Beat in the States, after another, American group, called The Beat – where are they now? – had threatened them with with a similar lawsuit). The other Bangs had heard of Miles Copeland's association with their rivals and smelt money – they asked $20,000 for the rights to the name. Since the girls didn't have the money, or the desire to fork it over even if they had, they changed their name. "We wanted to keep the root word and it was better than anything else we came up with," Vicki later explained. "Adding on any prefixes made it sound silly, but adding on LES made it mean something else. It means to hang loose."
"And of course there was an Electric Prunes song called 'Bangles', which was very influential in making that decision," added Susanna. So The Bangs became The Bangles, gave up their menial day jobs and hit the road.

"It was a very good tour for us because we were thrown on it when we weren't quite ready for it," Vicki later told **Melody Maker**'s David Fricke. "We grew up very fast in the art of getting back at crowds. A lot of times people would just look at us and yell, 'Get off the stage, we want The Beat'. It was tough to play to that."

The Bangles also found themselves swept up into a movement (of sorts) – the aforementioned 'paisley underground': "For the most part we met through each other's music," Vicki later told David Fricke. "We'd get together and talk about records nobody else had – Syd Barrett doing Italian folk songs, that kind of thing. We were interested in it because it seemed eclectic and nobody else was into it at the time. There were still bands in LA doing Knack covers. But it got very complicated. I used to room

with Steve Wynn of The Dream Syndicate and I remember sitting down with him one day and saying, 'Do we like each other because we like each other's bands?' " Debbi Peterson also once shared a flat with Syd Griffin from The Long Ryders.

□ Susanna: "LA was basically rockabilly and hardcore punk and then all of a sudden bands like us, The Dream Syndicate and The Rain Parade started putting these little independent records out which got airplay from people like Rodney Bingenheimer. It was real different, it was song orientated; each band had a certain style that wasn't The Stray Cats or hardcore. Bands like The Three O'Clock, The Bangles, The Rain Parade and The Dream Syndicate are all very different sounding, but I think we inspired each other and it was really fun doing shows together."

To subsequent accusations that the paisley underground had been little more than a simple case of sixties revivalism, Vicki later replied, "They would all say that they weren't sixties bands. Although we all derive certain influences from the sixties, we're not trying to create a sound now that is sixties-ish. I don't think it's a case of being a sixties copyist band. I see it more as taking and building on the rock 'n' roll spirit that comes from that period."

□ In early 1983, Annette Zilinskas left to join cowpunk band Blood On The Saddle, and The Bangles found themselves needing a new bassist. They found her (there was no real question that it would be a 'her' rather than a 'him'; the girls had all played with male musicians as well, but preferred the all-girl scenario. Not that it was a feminist issue; for The Bangles feminism has always been taken for granted, rather than an 'issue') in the person of Michael Steele ('Mickey' to her friends), Vicki's then current room-mate.

☐ **MICHAEL STEELE** had grown up in Newport Beach, California, and had moved to Los Angeles at the age of 21. The daughter of Tommy (the owner of a chain of car-washes) and Nancy (an ex-commercial pilot), Michael had been an introverted teenager, who'd stayed in her room reading and drawing, "listening to the radio and having a rich fantasy life" . . . until she discovered the bass guitar. She was playing in her boyfriend Jim's band when producer Kim Fowley approached her and asked her to join a new all-girl rock band he was putting together. This was to be The Runaways, Fowley's teenage leather dream band (which would later unleash Joan Jett upon the world). The Runaways went through a whole host of lead singers in those early (pre-recording) days: Michael was one of them, and the experience soured her on the idea of all-girl groups. "After four months I got kicked out. Kim played this song 'Cherry Bomb' to me, and I said, 'Kim, I can't sing this, it's *stupid*.' That was the end of my career as a Runaway. It was a great education – it taught me all the things I didn't want to do.

"After that band I thought, 'I hate all-girl bands. I'll never do this again. This is the stupidest thing I've ever done'." But while working in a record shop Michael heard the first album by Cheap Trick – "Sort of heavy metal Beatles. I suddenly realised that I wanted to do it again, so I moved back to Hollywood, gritted my teeth and started playing in bands." *Lots* of bands. ("School of hard knocks. Hands-on experience! This is my 15th band. I'm serious. Including high school bands. I counted one day.") Among the 15 were Slow Children, Snakefinger, Tony And The Movers, Elton Duck, Greg Best, Boys Ranch, Rampage, Twister . . .

Finally, Michael heard through the grapevine of a room for rent in Vicki Peterson's house, *plus* the chance of a bass slot in The Bangles, and she decided to try and overcome her bias against girl groups.

"I really liked The Bangles, and I wanted to get in the band, so for one of the few times in my life, I made a totally calculated move and moved in with Vicki." Upon Zilinskas' resignation, Michael was auditioned and hired. Regarding her male-sounding first name, Steele has this to say: "I guess it's not as normal as 'Pam'. I changed my name in 1976 and, no, I'm not going to tell you what it was before. It wasn't a horrible name or anything – I changed it for personal reasons." When (after finding fame and fortune) the **Sun** newspaper wanted to know the reason for Michael's name, "We thought, 'This is great. We'll tell them it's a sex change because it was the only way I could get into the band'."

"I used to be a cashier at a car wash, Susanna worked in a factory making jewellery, Vicki and Debbi worked in this American art museum and Debbi even worked briefly at a McDonalds. So we've all had weird jobs – and playing music may be crazy but it's a *whole* lot nicer."
☐ Michael

□ By now The Bangles mini-album had been released, and had attracted a fair amount of attention. Several majors were courting the group; eventually CBS succeeded, and signed them to a three-album deal.

The first fruit of this was 'All Over The Place', released in March 1985, and a vast improvement on the EP. Produced by David Kahne, the album showed The Bangles' talents to the full. It was pop with bounce, which paid unashamed homage to the folkier side of West Coast sixties rock, with Byrdsian guitars and vocal harmonies (lead vocals were pretty evenly shared between Susanna and the Peterson sisters) reminiscent of The Mamas And Papas (or in this case, The Mamas And The Mamas, as somebody pointed out). The lyrics were witty, even literate ('Dover Beach' even references T. S. Eliot's 'The Love Song Of J. Alfred Prufrock') and the general mood was one of positive upfullness. The first single off the album, 'Hero Takes A Fall' attracted a fair amount of attention, and the rest of the album was as easy on the ear as the girls' appearance was on the eye.

Considering the album's limited budget, there was quite a bit of experimentation going on too, as in the orchestrated ballad 'More Than Meets The Eye'.

In addition to nine Bangles originals, the album also featured two cover versions: sixties group The Merry Go-Round's 'Live', and 'Going Down To Liverpool', written by Kimberley Rew (who had just left The Soft Boys, and was then recording demos with his new band, Katrina And The Waves). The song was an ode to the dubious joys of the dole queue and the bleakness of the English job market – it *sounded* incredibly joyful, until you heard the lyrics. Not only does the song's protagonist have a UB40 in his/her hand, but he/she fully expects to be doing 'nothing, for the rest of my life.' Cheerful stuff, and right on the money for a British audience, even if it was written by an American.

Vicki and Michael had stumbled across the song in demo form, and were knocked out by its simplicity and the fact that "something about the guitars sounded like us." It was released as the album's second single, and though the video for the song bore no relevance to the song's lyrics, it did feature an extraordinary guest star: Leonard Nimoy, aka **Star Trek**'s Mr Spock (a friend of the Hoffs family). "He was really into the idea," Vicki told **Record Mirror**'s Robin Smith. "It was something completely different for him and he had a great time. Apparently he was in a rock band himself back in the sixties. We all like **Star Trek**. One of my room-mates was a real Trekkie; she even changed her name to Spock." The song had inevitably attracted a certain amount of attention in England, but on the eve of their first English tour Susanna told **Sounds**' Edwin Pouncey, "I don't think I feel compelled to go to Liverpool. It doesn't mean I love The Beatles any less, it's just the way I look at it. I can't feel that I have to go there." The song finally became a hit in Britain when it was re-released in the wake of the success of 'Manic Monday' and 'If She Knew What She Wants'.

If the commercial success of 'All Over The Place' was slight, it had at least attracted some critical acclaim, and The Bangles had begun to build a new live following wherever they played. "It did just what we wanted in that it broke through to other markets that hadn't heard us before," said Vicki. "We had a club following and a lot of good press in LA, but we had to go further than that."

And the success was more than welcome, as Michael pointed out: "We're selling out. It took a long time, and we've been waiting for it a long time." "We're not a garage band any more," said Vicki. "We're a living room band now."

□ They were especially pleased by their live achievements, and the new audiences they'd conquered. "We'd been warned about the response of UK audiences, about them being very conservative," said Vicki, "so we were really surprised at how wonderful the response was."

"That's what's so great about playing concerts to all these adolescents – it's like they're right in the midst of it," said Susanna. "It's like you never grow up fully, you always carry with you the scars of adolescence. Rock 'n' roll seems to make it feel better."

Of course, The Bangles' appeal wasn't simply an aural one; in keeping with their sixties approach, they'd always dressed the part. But while hippie splendour (and more importantly, mini-skirts) were ideal for attracting the attention of teenage boys (and older ones too), their clothing could have its drawbacks. "We think we look normal, but obviously we don't, 'cause we get stopped at airports and frisked and glanced at as if we were from another planet," complained Michael. "It really is weird when somebody goes through your underwear and stockings and stuff," added Susanna. "I said, 'What are you going to find in there? Pills?' It was very humiliating, very embarrassing."

But despite the girls' background in psychedelic music, and though they all admit to having experimented with "certain substances" in the past, by 1986 (possibly even earlier) The Bangles were all drug-free, and strongly against substance abuse. Debbi barely even drank. But then again, the paisliest person of them all was also vehemently anti-drugs, and he was about to enter their world and change it forever.

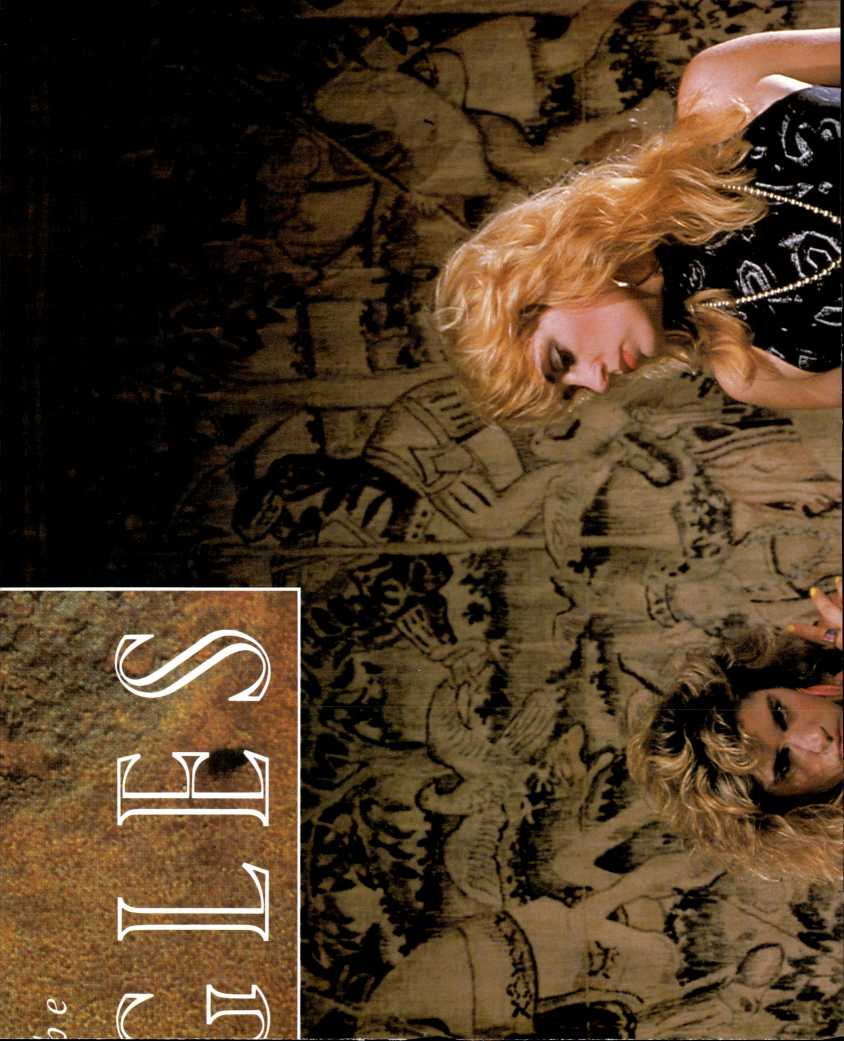

"We're trying to recapture a sound which was popular before the laser rock and big stadium acts of the seventies. It's just a simpler, purer sound. We aren't the only band doing that : in America there's REM, and in Britain you have The Smiths."
□ Susanna

☐ Susanna Hoffs first met His Impish Indigoness (copyright Caren Myers 1988) aka The Mauve Monarch Of Minneapolis, Prince himself – in 1984, when he came to a backstage Bangles party, though their tryst was cut short when one of his managers announced that it was midnight and time to go. "Just like Cinderella, eh?" said Susanna. "What happens at midnight?" "Oh," Prince replied, "the bodyguards turn into rats."

Whether or not Prince's interest in La Hoffs was personal or professional has since been the subject of much speculation. Some reports allege that he called her often; he certainly came to see several Bangles shows, even occasionally joining the band on-stage.

Prince would certainly have found The Bangles much to his taste, quite apart from the fact that Susanna was very much in the mould of 'Prince's women'. He'd achieved his greatest success to date with **Purple Rain**, a film/album that plumbed much of the same psychedelic territory as The Bangles' world. For whatever reason, he decided to give them a demo tape of two of his unreleased songs for them to cover: 'Manic Monday' and 'Jealous Girl'. The latter remains unreleased (by either party), while the former was an almost perfect pop song that would – with a little help from MTV and radio airplay – catapult The Bangles onto a far wider stage.

The song was credited to 'Christopher' (Prince having a fondness for pseudonyms), Christopher Tracy being the name of the character he was about to play in his new movie, **Under The Cherry Moon** (possibly the worst film ever made, but at least it proved that there was *something* – i.e. acting – that Prince *wasn't* able to do immaculately). It's probable that the song was an old one that Prince pulled out of his legendary stockpile: for one thing, it sounds nothing like the material Prince was about to release on the 'Parade' album; for another, the verse section is almost identical to that of '1999', Prince's 1983 hit.

"Prince must have written them with us in mind," Hoffs told **No 1**'s Max Bell. "We didn't have to change them much. 'Manic Monday' didn't even need the sex roles changing around. It's a sexy but very feminine song. Our version is like Jimi Hendrix meets The Velvet Underground meets The Mamas And Papas." Conversely, Vicki claimed that, "We made a few changes and did it our way, but I think you can still tell that it's a Prince melody. I think he liked the fact that we used a little bit of licence with it." "He really is immersed in a creative state of mind all the time," Susanna added, awestruck.

Michael told **Smash Hits**' Tom Hibbert: "He just seems fascinated with women, uh, women making music. So he submitted the song and came to watch us playing it in rehearsal. That was real nerve-wracking: we're standing there playing and he's lying right there on the couch . . . he's a little crispy round the edges."

Nevertheless, 'Manic Monday' boded well for the album to follow. Nor was that the end of the Prince connection; in January 1986 the girls were invited to a party to hear a preview of the 'Parade' album, and Susanna was presented with a huge yellow guitar-shaped birthday cake. At the end of 1986 he joined them on-stage at a Los Angeles show and they went back to the studio with him afterwards, playing Bangles music ("he knew all our songs") till three the next morning. "You know those kids who are like five years old and they have absolutely no fear of falling, and they're the best skiers? That's kinda what Prince was like when we jammed with him," explained Susanna to **Melody Maker**'s Carol Clerk.

□ But Prince's attentions drew the eyes of the media to the group in general, and to Susanna in particular. Prince was good newspaper copy, and the papers wanted to know all the tawdry details (assuming there were any); nor would they leave the thing alone. It reached the point where many thought that it was creating a rift between Susanna and the other girls. She'd always been the centre of attention to some extent, largely because she was so petite. At five-foot-two she was almost a foot shorter than the others; she stood out in photos, almost always occupying the foreground. And then, there were those big, big eyes . . .

Susanna's own comment on Prince's interest in her was that it was "very mysterious"; of the media attention she commented, "I think I can't change the way the world perceives the band. There's someone in The Bangles for everybody. What we do is a collaboration. You can't take out any member of the band and still have The Bangles. I think there's room within The Bangles organization for everything."

□ The others had their own problems, with the media and with the pressures of success. "It's nice that people are interested," Michael told **Rolling Stone**'s Steve Pond, "but it's rough when all of a sudden you don't have any time off. I mean, *boy* bands don't have to worry about putting on makeup in the morning and looking good all day long." Getting up early and having hardly any privacy were common complaints; the constant touring would also cause all of them to break up with their boyfriends. "We go to all these fabulous places. Just fabulous. They're so romantic. We have all these wonderful romantic meals with . . . no one," complained Susanna. "We're staying in these picturesque Swiss chalets and there's no one there. I just wish that we could share it sometimes with some guy, you know."

"Me and Mickey are into micro-mini-skirts.
I'm also going through a Spanish dancer phase;
I like all my dresses to have huge ruffs."
☐ Susanna

With A-Ha

□ For The Bangles were becoming *hugely* popular, in the wake of their new album and the follow-up singles to 'Manic Monday' (to which we shall address ourselves in a moment). And on top of all their other problems, by early the following year Susanna was set to become a film star, in **Cutting Loose** (originally titled **The Allnighter**), a teen angst romance written and directed by her mother which also starred Joan Cusack and Michael Ontkar. Tamar Hoffs described her daughter as "the ultimate star" (in the event, the film made little impact), and Susanna herself said, "There are so many things I want to do in this life, and The Bangles is just one of them. I give it my all, but it's just something that I do." This from a girl who a year earlier had told **Record Mirror**, "With rock 'n' roll, you call the shots, you write the script, design the costumes. You're everything. And it's such a fun, free, rebellious art form."

But privacy – in terms of dodging the paparazzi – was fairly easy. "You just wear something you wouldn't wear on-stage and you're all right," said Vicki. "I pull my hair back, put on my glasses and there's no problem." "With me, people never think I'm in The Bangles 'cause I'm so petite," Susanna added. "They say, 'You're so tiny I don't see how you can be Susanna'."

But there was a good side to the fame as well. They got to meet the more famous of their new fans, who included some heroines and heroes of their own: Joni Mitchell, James Taylor, Michael J. Fox, Robert Plant (who thought they were "refreshing") and Sting. They were even asked to write a song for the reunion (minus Mike Nesmith) album of The Monkees. Though The Monkees "ended up going into the studio before we had a chance to get together with them," said Vicki, they did meet the group later at an awards ceremony. "That was a thrill," Vicki continued. "I was sitting in a room putting on some lipstick or something, and I looked over and there was Davy Jones drying his hair with a towel! I heard his voice, and I thought, 'Oh my God – I had a crush on this guy when I was six-years-old!' "

□ But the album that was causing all the fuss, 'Different Light' had been a painful, problematical

one to record. They were once again teamed with producer David Kahne, who told **Rolling Stone** that he'd "wanted more variety in the writing. I thought if they had some songs that were a little bit more fundamental rhythmically – not quite so antsy – and if they sang the normal way they sing, they might get on the radio." This the girls reluctantly agreed to; they'd been touring non-stop to promote 'All Over The Place', and the songs they'd managed to stockpile were not among their strongest. So they settled on eight Bangle originals, and Kahne and the girls then listened to over one hundred 'outside' tunes (Vicki: "He'd bring in things that other people at the label thought would be good for us, and we'd just crack up after four seconds") before deciding on Jules Shear's 'If She Knew What She Wants', Alex Chilton's 'September Gurls' (originally recorded by Big Star) and Liam Sternberg's 'Walk Like An Egyptian'. (Sternberg knew a thing or two about girl singers, having figured heavily in the early careers of Jane Aire and Rachel Sweet.)

Though none of the girls were exactly over the moon with the finished album, they played the party line. "We had that sort of Top 40 programmer thing on our mind when we went into the studio," said Susanna, "but, in the end, I don't think we've had to compromise our sound at all. The band have just grown up as people while we've been playing together."

Overall, the sound this time was lusher, and benefited from being fleshed-out with keyboards. And even Michael got to sing, taking lead vocals on her own jazzy 'Following', as well as on the exquisite 'September Gurls'.

The quaintly eccentric 'Walk Like An Egyptian' shot straight to the top of the charts, aided by a video in which the girls – glammed to the hilt in Cleopatra rig-outs – were intercut with the general public (looking pretty downbeat), all of them 'walking like Egyptians' (which may well be a slur on Egyptians). But one person who hated the song however, was Debbi Peterson. She neither sang nor played on the song, which she dismissed as "a nice little novelty song kind of thing, but I don't feel it's us." Debbi had been unable to get along with Kahne from the start, and had requested a change of producer (and been outvoted) quite early in the proceedings.

Ironically, Kahne *had* been right to bring in outside writers, but that meant that the album's strength was also its weakness, since the cover versions were far stronger than The Bangles originals. Only Susanna's 'Walking Down Your Street' could truly hold its head up, succeeding in its own right as a single.

With TerenceTrent D'Arby

"Madonna and Cyndi Lauper's live shows are mostly women. At our concerts we get a ridiculous number of boys. Maybe we're giving off a different sexual energy."
□ Susanna

□ But despite the hits, life was still pretty basic, as Michael told **Melody Maker**'s Helen Fitzgerald: "Three-quarters of this band is basically homeless. Well, how can you put down $400 when you're not getting a salary? You either sub-let your apartment when you're touring or you move – and we've moved every single tour. We're *always* juggling money."

Somehow, they managed to beat the media down; they were determined not to be treated as bimbos-of-the-month. Michael told **Rolling Stone**, "We just want people to realise that we're not models, we're not actresses, we're not some sixties act, and we're not a cute little novelty. We're a rock 'n' roll band, and that's the way we want to be treated."

In the end, 'Different Light' sold over a million copies worldwide, while the singles from the album totalled sales of over two million. Proud of their native daughters' success, Los Angeles (through Mayor Tom Bradley) designated February 23, 1987 as 'Bangles Day'.

But as far as Kahne was concerned, it was too late. He was informed that he would not be producing the follow-up; though disappointed he conceded that 'Different Light' had been "a very difficult record for them to make. Whenever something good happens

With Kevin Costner

time to time but really, people tend to overplay our relationship," Debbi told the **NME**'s Sean O'Hagan. "He's a pretty maladjusted guy," added Michael. "He operates in a cocoon and is real uncomfortable with outsiders. He records and plays all the time. That's his whole life." Thank you and goodnight, Mr Nelson.

☐ It was time to start thinking seriously about the next album. But first – along with Run DMC, Aerosmith, Slayer, Joan Jett and Roy Orbison, The Bangles had agreed to contribute a track to the soundtrack of **Less Than Zero**, the movie of the Brett Easton Ellis novel about the cocaine lifestyle in Hollywood. They chose to cover a Paul Simon song, 'A Hazy Shade Of Winter' (from the Simon And Garfunkel 'Bookends' album), a song they'd played live back in the club days which "kinda matched the bleakness of the film."

Recording it was, if not a bleak experience, certainly a difficult one. Removed from Kahne and "away from the people we'd sort of been nurtured by, or thought we were dependent on," the girls were stuck with an unsympathetic producer in Rick Rubin, and ended up pretty much producing themselves. When asked about Rubin, Susanna told Sean O'Hagan, "He's OK. I wouldn't like to have to do an album with him. I'd rather work with a producer who is actually *there* in the studio when you're recording." "He was always over the road in The Rainbow, which is a huge metal hang-out," added Vicki. "He has a different attitude," Hoffs went on, "kind of, let's do it *fast*. He wanted to put out a version that was real unfinished, but we went back into the studio without him and overdubbed for two days . . ." "Then he disowned it," interrupted Vicki. "He *hated* the finished version, thought it was too *homo*. That's his favourite word – *homo* – for anything that ain't macho enough for Rick Rubin." Clearly not the happiest of relationships.

Nor did they have too much faith in the movie. Vicki: "The book was bogus. That guy was trying to be *so* cool all the time but it just came out inane and vacuous, a real hoot. The book didn't work and I don't think the movie does either." She added that, "If it's an anti-drug movie, I'm all for it," but it didn't exactly sound like a plug.

But the song – a pleasant, and surprisingly faithful cover version – ended up faring far better than the movie (which pretty much died). Its success was just the shot in the arm they needed, as they prepared to enter the studio with new producer Davitt Sigurson. This time they knew what they wanted.

on a record, there's been some suffering. After going through that with someone, you don't always want to do it again. They were insecure, and learning can be very scary."

"I feel very detached from the record in a lot of ways," was how Vicki summed up her feelings. "I want the next album to be a little more of what The Bangles are on-stage – a little more rock 'n' roll, a little more guitar oriented. I feel very strongly about using our songs."

☐ In February 1988 the girls flew into Britain to attend the BPI awards and appear on **Wogan**. The BPI is generally considered to be merely a self-congratulatory waste of time on the part of the record industry. Two years earlier they'd flown over and Susanna had sat next to Prince on the plane, renewing the friendship that would lead to so much success and so much trouble. This time there were few friendly faces around, and they were asked whether this was a real drag or what. "It's real Elk Lodge stuff," said Vicki. "Y'know, pretty lame and boring and totally based on sales as opposed to merit. It's part of playing the game. Being visible. We call it the Miss America syndrome."

Naturally, they were still being asked questions about Prince. "We keep bumping into him from

□ Susanna: "We trusted ourselves and our ideas about arrangements, about harmonies, about tempo, about musicianship." Debbi: "Everyone threw out a lot of ideas and nearly all of them got used. We had a lot more freedom on this record and did a lot of things that added both to the music and to the fun level. We're really proud of this album, and really excited about it. We put a lot of work into it, and a lot of heart, because we wanted it to be special."

The one aspect that they wanted above all to be 'special' was the song content. This time (though each of the girls would work with outside collaborators), no cover versions would be recorded and no outside songwriting teams would be used: each song would be a Bangles original. They were obviously determined to prove that they could write. "We decided from the beginning, 'OK, it's the songwriting Olympics – everyone write to your heart's content'," recalls Debbi. "So we all went off on our own and went on a complete songwriting spree."

And the good news is that it paid off. Whilst 'Everything' contains its fair share of fillers among the 13 tracks (Vicki: "More Bangles for your buck!"), the strong tracks are as catchy as any of the singles from 'Different Light'. The first single off the album, 'In Your Room', couldn't really fail; what red-blooded teenage boy could resist Susanna Hoffs' offer: 'I'll do anything you want me to, in your room'? Plus it had bounce; as Susanna pointed out, "It's got the Tommy James-style Hammond organ with a little bit of that eighties Fat Boy/Prince thing."

Susanna also contributed the ethereal 'Waiting For You', while the Peterson sisters weighed in with 'The Bell Jar', a tip of the hat to Sylvia Plath's novel. Solo, Debbi provided the ballad 'Be With You' (which would be the third single), and Vicki supplied the plaintive 'Make A Play For Her Now' and the driving rocker 'Crash And Burn', which was co-written with Rachel Sweet and sounds exactly like Wreckless Eric playing with Blondie. Michael's 'Glitter Years' was a bitter-sweet ode to the glam excesses of the early seventies and featured a creditable imitation of Ziggy-era Bowie.

□ But the jewel in the album's crown was 'Eternal Flame', a sweeping ballad of undying love (a torch song, in fact; sorry 'bout that one) from Susanna, to which producer Sigurson gave "the orchestrated kind of production Owen Bradley would have done for Patsy Cline in 1959." As playground lovers prepared to separate for the summer of 1989, the song was released as a single, and became a runaway smash;

"Madonna's ridiculous. Her success seems to be based on how many clothes she's able to take off. The Bangles are very sexual on stage and we sing sexual music, but we don't think it's necessary to dress up in flimsy clothes to get the message across. I guess we're more subtle."
□ Vicki

"Our first record was all about, 'If your man gives you shit then *dump* him, don't let him spoil your life.' Now it's like, 'God, I'm so in love.' Our feelings haven't really changed, we've just grown up a bit now and we're getting to think of the, um, *romantic side of romance*."
□ Susanna

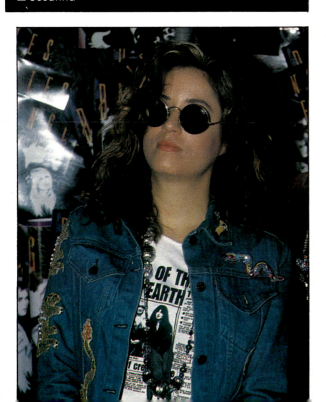

it topped the British charts for over a month, even without a promotional visit.

The story behind the song Susanna explained to TV's **Rapido**: "I wrote it with some friends, Billy Steinberg and Tom Kelly. I was over at Billy's house and we were working on songs, and I told him about The Bangles going to Gracelands, Elvis' house, on a tour. It was raining and we went to the backyard where everybody's buried from the family. Michael noticed at the head of Elvis' grave this plexiglass box that was filled with rainwater. She asked the tour guide, 'What's that?', and he said, 'Well, that's the eternal flame'." Which begs the question, 'How eternal is eternal?' . . . but enough of philosophy.

□ When they finally came within hailing distance of English reporters (in Amsterdam, where they visited a live sex show, that being one of the things you have to do in Amsterdam, whether you're a Bangle or not), they were (inevitably) asked about acid house, the current musical flavour of the month. When Susanna (accurately) observed, "That's not acid – that's bad disco," somebody should have given her a medal.

□ Asked about the new songs, Michael replied, "All the songs are autobiographical. We write about a lot of personal stuff." "I like writing about people," added Vicki. "I like writing about relationships, that's important to me. The way we treat each other, even on a one-to-one basis, is just as important as the starving in Africa."

To **Melody Maker**'s Caroline Sullivan, Vicki explained further: "It's a dangerous thing for us to have a political stance. We're four individuals and we have different ideas. We don't hold meetings every Monday night and say, 'What's happened during the week?' so we can give our views to the press, because who gives a shit? It's not what we write about. It's not that we're stupid and don't think about it, but we prefer to write about things of the heart. Social politics, about what people do to each other, men and women who relate to each other."

Added Debbi: "There are no drug rehab stories here, no lurid headlines, no photographer bashing. We're at a point now where we're writing about experiences, or people, we know – we're not into any heavy-duty political themes or big statements."

They also told of jamming with – of all people – The Grateful Dead. "Isn't it cool?" enthused Susanna. "We did 'Knockin' On Heaven's Door' and 'Iko Iko'. I've always loved them. Especially in college and stuff."

And they came up with an interesting variation on the meaning of the name 'The Bangles': "In Austrian it means 'wild boys', which we like a lot," said Vicki. "We like to hang loose with wild boys," Susanna giggled.

☐ Which brings us neatly onto the subject of romance. Vicki (ever the planner) had long ago pencilled Bangles Baby Year in for 1995. The plan was to have a big party and all conceive on the same night. Not that motherhood would spell the end of the group; as Vicki pointed out, "That never seems to end careers these days." "There is a continuing debate about the matter," Susanna once confirmed. "Lots of bands we know these days take their wives and kids on the road – but how many of them have to dance, leap, sing, and play guitar or drums when they're six months pregnant? Chrissie Hynde is the first obviously pregnant woman we've seen play rock 'n' roll."

The current contestants for Bangles fatherhood? Susanna is involved with Donovan Leitch the actor (son of Donovan Leitch the hippie balladeer), whom she affectionately refers to as Dono. "It's really a normal, sweet relationship. We're pretty serious, but I don't know if we're going to tie the knot." Debbi has recently married the group's road manager. Vicki's current romantic status is unknown, while Michael's last reported dalliance was two years ago, when she was linked with a member of Australian band The Hoodoo Gurus. It would appear that Bangle babies may be on schedule for a 1995 birth; then again, they may not.

☐ Meanwhile, they've got an album to promote. Summer 1989 saw them start a nationwide tour of the States, and **Rolling Stone**'s Holly Gleason was on hand at the tour's start in Santa Monica to stick the knife in. After bemoaning the fact that the age of the band's following (mainly young teenagers) was a drawback for a band trying to be taken seriously, and criticising the girls for clichéd guitar posturing, Gleason took the group to task for failing to break down rock's sexual fences. "The Bangles must still deal with rock's double standard," concluded Gleason, "by which women who are performers are expected to be cute playthings. Their attempts to take a hard line – such as a stage aside about what they want from 'their dudes' – remain largely unconvincing."

☐ So what's the final verdict on The Bangles? Ditzy dolly birds or complicated girls? I'd say the latter, probably. As to whether they're candy floss or protein, musically speaking . . . the answer is almost certainly both – and there's nothing wrong with that. At the time of 'Different Light' it would have been easy to dismiss them as just one more eighties mayfly band: a couple of good singles and that's your lot. Susanna would have gone on to a successful solo career, and it would have been The Go-Go's all over again.

Instead, The Bangles have genuinely tried. They've stood up for what they wanted, have honed their songwriting talents, and have refused to let their management package them or the media categorise them. They have refused to be dismissed as just another bunch of fizzy pop bimbos. If they use session musicians, what of it? At least they *can* play, and sing; and they never claimed to be anything more than a garage band anyway. If they've plundered the sixties, at least they've done so with immense good taste . . . and more than a little wit. Like Blondie or Nick Lowe, they've held up a mirror to the past and refracted the images in a way that spells h-i-t to a later generation, and that's no mean achievement.

☐ As I write, **The Guinness Book Of Records** lists Bananarama as the world's all-time most successful girl group, and I think that's a sad, bad joke. Given that The Crystals, The Ronettes, The Chiffons and The Shirelles are now all out of the running, I'd like to think that The Bangles will someday fill that slot. The way they're going, it shouldn't take them too long, either.

ALBUMS

☐ **BANGLES**

Side One:
The Real World/ I'm In Line/ Want You

Side Two:
Mary Street/ How Is The Air Up There?

Produced by Craig Leon.
IRS Records. IRS SP70506, 1982.

☐ **ALL OVER THE PLACE**

Side One:
Hero Takes A Fall/ Live/ James/ All About You/ Dover Beach

Side Two:
Tell Me/ Restless/ Going Down To Liverpool/ He's Got A Secret/ Silent Treatment/ More Than Meets The Eye

Produced and engineered by David Kahne.
CBS Records. CBS 450091, 1, March 1985.

☐ **DIFFERENT LIGHT**

Side One:
Manic Monday/ In A Different Light/ Walking Down Your Street/ Walk Like An Egyptian/ Standing In The Hallway/ Return Post

Side Two:
If She Knew What She Wants/ Let It Go/ September Gurls/ Angels Don't Fall In Love/ Following/ Not Like You

Produced by David Kahne.
CBS Records. CBS 26659, March 1986.

☐ **EVERYTHING**

Side One:
In Your Room/ Complicated Girl/ Bell Jar/ Something To Believe In/ Eternal Flame/ Be With You

Side One:
Glitter Years/ I'll Set You Free/ Watching The Sky/ Some Dreams Come True/ Make A Play For Her Now/ Waiting For You/ Crash And Burn

Produced by Davitt Sigerson.
CBS Records, CBS 462979 1, November 1988.

BANGLES FAN CLUB
**Bangles 'N' Mash
International Fan Club,
4455, Torrance Boulevard,
Suite 4455,
Torrance
CA 90503
USA**

(Include a SAE)

SINGLES

Getting Out Of Hand/ (B-Side Unknown)
(Downkiddie)

Hero Takes A Fall/ Where Were You When I Needed You
(CBS A4257)

Going Down To Liverpool/ Dover Beach/ The Real World/ I'm In Line/ How Is The Air Up There
(CBS TX4914)

Going Down To Liverpool/ Dover Beach
(CBS A4914)

Hero Takes A Fall/ Where Were You/ Manic Monday/ In A Different Light/ Going Down To Liverpool/ Dover Beach
(CBS TX6796)

Manic Monday/ In A Different Light
(CBS A6796)

If She Knew What She Wants/ Angels Don't Fall In Love
(CBS A7062: two 12″ versions released, the first including Manic Monday, the second including Hero Takes A Fall and James)

Going Down To Liverpool/ Let It Go
(CBS A7255: 12″ version includes Walking Down Your Street and James)

Walk Like An Egyptian/ Not Like You
(CBS 650071/6: two 12″ versions released, the first including two extra mixes of Egyptian, the second including Manic Monday and In A Different Light)

Walking Down Your Street/ Return Post
(BANGS 1: double single version includes Walk Like An Egyptian and Not Like You)

Following/ Dover Beach
(BANGS 2)

A Hazy Shade Of Winter/ She's Lost You
(BANGS 3)

In Your Room/ Bell Jar
(BANGS 4; 12″ version includes A Hazy Shade Of Winter)

Eternal Flame/ What I Meant To Say
(BANGS 5; 12″ version includes What I Meant To Say)

Be With You/ Let It Go
(BANGS 6; 12″ version includes In Your Room)